STORIES OF MY EXISTENTIAL LIFE

A poetry collection by O.B. Thompson

3rd Edition

© 2021 Oliver Thompson. All rights reserved.

Text © 2014, Oliver Thompson.
Photo © Scopio.

Third edition published by Warmbreeze Digital Publishing, 2021

First Edition published in 2012
Second Edition published in 2014

The words and images found in this book may not be reproduced without the express written consent of their respective owners.

Contents

Authors Notes	7
Stories of my Existential Life I: The Fear	9
Unflattering Words	10
Home Comforts	11
Nothing	11
The Six O'Clock News	12
Zombie State of Mind	12
Not Now	13
Man in the Mirror	14
A Kick in the Face for Hope	14
A Whirlwind Romance	15
Time of Death	16
Majesty	17
Missing	18
1:07 a.m.	18
Keys	19
For Jamie	19
The Clown	20
Back at the Ball Game	21
Stories of my Existential Life II: The Nihilist	22
Costly	23
Nelson, Madiba	23
Opening Eyes	24
Ninety Six	25
Burn Me	26
Drawn	26
Storm in a Teacup	27

Ghost Town	28
The Woman	29
The Day I Died	30
Simplistic Confusion	31
That Mysterious Woman	32
The Sparrow	33
9:58 p.m.	34
This Poem Has No Title and No Meaning	34
Breeding idiots	35
Older and Wiser	36
In Contradiction	37
Foghorns	38
Proverb	39
Soul in a Jar	39
Think	40
The Night	40
Rise & Fall	41
Warning	42
Pearl	43
Unfinished	44
Temporary Lover	45
A Question	46
Stories of my Existential Life III: Looking Forward	47

Authors Notes

Looking back on this collection it strikes me as overly dreary and depressing. I was recently told that the re-designed book cover for this collection looked "very depressing" too. I don't really know what that says about me but there we go. It's never been my intention to write poetry that can be interpreted this way but looking back at my own creative process it's easy to see why.

I would like to say that the 8 years that have passed since I first put pen to paper on the beginning of this collection have brought about a sunnier disposition on my part. But as I prepare to release another batch of new poetry into the world, it has become obvious that this is not the case.

It has been a challenging period in time for all, not just myself and it is strange to me now that so much of what's contained in this collection could so easily have been written this year as opposed to eight years ago. The same feelings of unease and loneliness still can still be traced to day to day life and we're all still angry about the same things.

Perhaps that means that the title of this collection is as appropriate as it ever was and that growing older is no assurance that those feelings will subside. I think it can also relate more generally to the world and the state we find ourselves in. We've never been more divided and each day seems to bring new questions about our own existence that we hadn't previously considered.

Are we all just telling stories of our own existential lives? Ask me again in another 8 years.

Stories of my Existential Life I: The Fear

I hope that I die when I'm tired of life.

I feel so alone; not that I'm lonely,
I'm in a room full of people.
Talking,
Laughing,
Being,
All the things that I am not.

When everyone's gone I'll be on my own;
I'll tell myself, fine, I was always alone.

I get confused sometimes as to what I'm doing here;
I look up not to search but to laugh and to cry;
Out of anger and out of fear.

These people keep yelling and I keep not listening,
Last time I listened I came somehow to cry,
When I try to listen they make the wrong sounds,
Nothing I can do but shy.

I rack my brain in search of truth;
The light makes things darker, not a little a bit clear;
I ask myself why am I human?
And why am I here?

Unflattering Words

A sordid criticism is nothing
To be taken lightly, if at all.
What remains is the droll ramblings
Of those whose pens remain untouched
And brains remain unused.

Somewhere out there is an idea.
Where?
I don't think I'll ever know;
But when you find it,
Be gentle.
Because that idea could save your life.

I'll keep writing lines of heresy;
Against your bureaucratic Satanism,
In the hope that you'll one day
Accept my amiable constructivism.

Home Comforts

Home is far too comfortable,
Yet comfort is our greatest fear,
And the comfort of home is overwhelming.
It's been a long time coming,
But now I have to leave once more.
I'd die just to feel alive again.

Nothing

Cave in to nothing, I dare you.
Render me speechless,
Render us worthless,
That's all it comes down to in the end.
Turning something to nothing,
But I think it's nothing to nothing.

Either way, who would know?
I certainly wouldn't.
And in the end, who would care?
I certainly wouldn't.

The Six O'Clock News

Once I had a halo but then it caught on fire.
Once I met a leader but then he committed genocide.
Once I met a deaf man but he was disgraced to hear that the world had turned to shit.

Zombie State of Mind

A zombie state of mind is hard to shake,
When everything moves so slowly,
And when everyone else is dead
On their feet too.

Nothing fits,
And nothing sits
Right in my mind anymore.
The world rushes by;
Walls shake as my fists pound them.

I'm scared.

Why can't I get out?
What's coming next?
God help me;
Because I need to believe in something.

Not Now

They didn't cut off my hands,
But I feel like I can't touch anything anymore.

They didn't cut off my ears;
But I feel like I can't hear anyone anymore.

Is this the way you're meant to feel?

It's been so long that I just don't know anymore.
How am I supposed to feel?

In a world that doesn't make sense,
There's nothing you can do for me,
Because you don't need me anymore.

I feel like I've been away for years,
But it's only been days;
I feel like I have no one,
When I've just pushed them away.

Man in the Mirror

I look in the mirror hung up on the door,
I say pleased to meet you, how do you do?
To the person I've not seen before.

You look like someone I used to know;
But I thought that he had died years ago.
Or at least I hoped he had.

It turns out that he never goes away.

A Kick in the Face for Hope

I've been dragged to the brink,
And brought right back again.
There's no shortcut to heaven,
But I thought I'd try anyway.

You never know,
Traffic might have been light that day.
Death is a natural part of life;
So I thought I'd get it out of the way.

You knocked on the door,
And I said I was busy;

All you wanted to know was what I wanted for my dinner.

A Whirlwind Romance

Young love is nothing new,
Especially when she is as pretty as you.
Full of life, full of soul,
Always talking, breathing in my ear on my Sunday stroll,
Some people say our love is strange.

The city that always sleeps.
The sleeping giant that lurks in.
The urban rainforest.

She is beautiful and I am not,
At least that's what I've been told.

I've never felt more at home.

Time of Death

Remember back when the world was flat?
The time of the divine autocrat,
And endless pious combat,
What happened to that?

We shame them as troglodytes,
Yet somehow they survived without the artificial lights,
And superficial sights,
That keep messing with my head.

It's simple anthropology,
That all this technology,
Is destroying our biology;
Yet I still don't hear an apology,
From the suits sitting on their neon ideology.
You don't need me to sit and spurt mindless terminology,
To know that when students of archaeology,
Find our toxicology;

It'll read: dead.

Majesty

If I could be anyone; I think I'd be a bird.
I could fly anywhere I wanted to,
Whenever I wanted to;
Rather than listening to the bus timetables;
Which seem hell bent on going at times
That I don't want them to.

Birds fly majestically,
I wait impatiently.

What's the point in walking anywhere?
When there are things to take us there.
A bird wouldn't have these problems,
Now you see,
Why it would be good to be a bird,
And not a person.
Although I suspect that I stopped
Being one of those a long time ago.

Do birds dream?
If not then I'd make an excellent bird;
I gave that up years ago too.

Missing

I wish people would stop
Telling me to plan for the future,
'You must care about the future!'
Why?
I might not even be around in the future.

Definitely not the way I'm going anyway.
I barely care about the present.

So why should I care about the future,
When the future doesn't care about me?

1:07 a.m.

The fall is further than the drop,
I'm clinging on for dear life,
Not that my life's worth much.

Might as well just let go then.

Keys

What good is a lock that has many keys?
No good.

It might work for a while,
But eventually,
You'd need a new lock;
One that's right for your key.
I guess some people are never happy.

For Jamie

Abundant creativity lights up the darkest room,
Every day is a chance to start anew,
Paint a picture with your words,
Write a beautiful melody,
Let your pictures speak a thousand words.

Trust yourself for no one knows you better;
Aim not to succeed but never to quit;
And give nothing but your best.

Be courageous, be true;
Most importantly, be you.

The Clown

I always thought I'd be the first to leave this town,
This dead rubber, backwater town.

I had plans to leave, to fly;
I wonder why
I never saw them through.

I always thought I'd be the first to leave,
But now I'm stuck here and time is turning quicker.
My time is up and I'm still stuck;
Destined to never fly the nest.

I am the ostrich that dared to dream.

I never wanted to be an ostrich,
How funny;
Maybe I am the clown, the sad clown.

Am I the sad clown in the sad town,
With the sad frown looking down,
At everything I wanted to be and wondering
'Where did it all go wrong?'
I am the clown who knew it was okay to be sad.

Do I have to be what everyone wants me to be?
After all I'm only me,
And I am free.
I still have time,
We all have time.

Back at the Ball Game

The scoreboard reads:

Bottom nine.
2 out;
3 on.

"Batter up!" comes the shout,

Way back in the stands sits a child effervescent with joy;
His father beside him speaks to him softly;
Close your eyes and think,
That could be me.

The roar of the throbbing crowd longing for victory
Seats teeming with fans
Some sad with worry, some happy with glee.

The scuffing of shoes,
The clearing of throats,
The build up to when pandemonium ensues.

That old smell of peanuts,
The roll of the organ,
The batter steps up to take his cuts.

He steps up to the plate,
Breathes; and takes it all in
He closes his eyes and thinks to himself;
Why me and not him?

Stories of my Existential Life II: The Nihilist

A man sits swinging his legs on the wooden bridge;
The ageing wood creaks beneath him,
As he shifts awkwardly from side to side;
His face as clear as the sky

The sun bounces from the rooftops,
Illuminating the silent fields below,
The wind blows the blossoming flowers gently;
The silent canal crinkles like paper in the gentle breeze

The scene is picturesque;
But the man has no camera.

He feels no joy, no sadness,
He feels no anger, no calm,
He feels no fear,
He feels nothing.

He is even more alive than you or I?

A solitary child is playing alone,
She smiles toward the man,
Perhaps even she feels pity for him.
I know I would,
I know I do.

Costly

Diamonds in her eyes,
Flowers in her hands,
I saw it end right then and there.

Tears of value roll down her blissful cheek,
Her heart of gold shatters.

Br*eaks.*
Falls.
Destroyed.

Never mind girl, there's always tomorrow.

Nelson, Madiba

The dark reveals true light,
Step forward luminescent;
Through courage, strength and fight;
Guide us home.

Uyindoda emadodeni
Kuwe Imvula iyana endlini
Enkosi kakhuli, Madiba
Ndiyakuthanda

Opening Eyes

All around me I see people living off greed,
Taking food from the mouths they're meant to feed.
All around me I see people living off war,
Pouring salt in the wounds of those still sore.

All around me I see people living off betrayal,
We are endless victims of a victimless portrayal.
All around me I see people living off lies,
Telling more to get ahead towards the unwinnable prize.

All around me I see people living off crime,
For all that you've stolen, you're wasting your time.

Nothing is reachable in this one-way world,
My broken heart is joylessly unfurled,
In one door and out the other,
Yet I still see people running for cover.

Ninety Six

A thousand lies were told,
About those who can't grow old.
Justice never rests and truth is always found,
The screaming of the kop in that famous old ground,
Will always be for justice to be done,
The battle for their loved ones has only just begun.

United we stand in times of great appal,
We put aside things as futile as football.

The dead had their voice taken,
We tried our best to bring it back,
And now the country's shaken;
To its bloody, rotten core.

In times of dark there's always light,
And for the good hard working people,
There's meaning in the fight,
For those who sobbed within that famous steeple.

Walk on with love and hope in your hearts,
Forever remembered within these parts.

And now I make a promise to you;
Those who lost their lives that day,
Because united we stand, red and blue;
Someone soon will pay.

Burn Me

O mighty temptress challenge me,
Upon thy hearty flame;
I've said it once that only it can be;
You that bares that task to tame
The ghost of you and me.

Extinguish me with thy breath,
I am a wounded flame;
Oh my faded heart shines but once;
Anxiously glowingly in the tenderness of your beauty.

I found nothing of myself in you;
But everything of you in me.

Drawn

I hate being drawn,
For it is not a pretty picture,
Especially when it does not concern me.

Death is an ugly mistress
Who paints no worse a picture;
But she will paint us all one day.
Some soon,
Some far,
But you cannot run away.

She paints with a single colour.

Storm in a Teacup

I hear the noise outside again,
The howling winds, the pouring rain.
It lashes down, innate, ferocious, without pity;
It beats the ground with an unrivalled ferocity.
The winds howl,
The sky is foul.

The sound grows louder by the second,
On the horizon does thunder beckon.
I love the sound.
I want the sound.
People say that they hate something that I have found.

So calming, so assuring.
Are they lying?
Or am I crazy?

Ghost Town

The lights ablaze with neon glow;
Pebbles, dusted with ice;
Frozen wasteland;
Industrial heaven;
Not a soul to die here,
This is the life of the party.

You speak in tongues,
For all else is foreign;
There's a ghost in this town,
Its name long forgotten;

He looks like you and talks like you;
You swear you've never seen him;
No one here knows your name.

Time to go;
Time to live.

The Woman

My shoulder made of lead,
From memories I've carried all these years,
Nothing needs to be said.
But then again does it ever?
And who is listening anyway?
Nobody ever listens to me
I cry, I beg, I plead!
But nobody ever listens to me.
The fact of the matter is that I would bleed
Before anyone would listen to me;
Yet I still continue talking.

To whom you may ask?
That is the question,
The question I cannot answer.
Yet I still continue talking,
To the woman behind the mask.

The woman stares at me,
I know she's laughing but I do not know why.
Sometimes it seems like she is crying,
But I do not know why.
Maybe I just convinced myself that it was okay to cry;
After all, why should I care who cries?
It's not as though anyone is listening.

Nobody ever listens,
And by then it is too late.

The Day I Died

I remember the day I died.

The birds cried out for me;
Half in pain,
Half in sorrow.

Like me, they fall to the earth flat on their face.
Will this feeling come again tomorrow?
Or will I shake its eerie grace?

Do you remember the day that I died?

Of course you don't,
Of course you won't.
Ignorance is bliss,
Just like a devil's kiss.

You said you'd never die,
As long as I'm alive.
Now I see that for what it was;
A filthy, rotten lie.

I wish I didn't remember the day I died.

Simplistic Confusion

They say that there are only two things,
That can satisfy any man,
I find that a bit too simplistic.

They say that only sex
And money can make a man happy.
I think they might be wrong.

Never have I met a man
More inclined by sex than solitude.
It seems men only want one thing;
To be left alone.

If it's all so simple,
Why am I struggling
To comprehend if this is even true?
Leave me alone for a minute and I'll tell you.

Sit hand in hand with one song in your heart,
If you can save yourself, at least that's a start.

That Mysterious Woman

I took a long walk today,
Down that long ramshackled old street,
Hidden from everyone that I could still see.
The flickering neon and restless candles
Seemed to guide me,
To that old café that I love so dear.
(The one with the apricot pastry)

The weary baker, who recognized me by now
Called out to me, he said
'Monsieur, what do you think of Paris?'
'Paris', I replied;
'Pourquoi elle est magnifique'
He chuckled
'Then why do you always look so sad?'
I chuckled;
'Because she is so beautiful.'

He said he did not understand;
So I spoke again.
He chuckled.
'I understand not your meaning.'
I laughed again,
I explained, partly in English,
Partly in French, but wholly in Truth;
*'How can one be happy,
When she is so beautiful and one is not?'*

Alas, he did not have an answer.

The Sparrow

There's a sparrow on my windowsill,
I don't know what it wants.

I look at its cold, dead eyes,
And I think that it doesn't want anything
But to annoy me.

It taps:

Once,
Twice,
Thrice.

I open the window;
It flies in and circles above my head.

How rude; I thought,
I ask it further questions,
Yet still it does not reply.

It swoops upon my shoulder,
And there it sits quite still.
It makes me feel much older,
Than people ever will.

9:58 p.m.

I turned to Satan because God wouldn't listen any more;
But in the end he shut me out;
I guess that eventually we all get tired;
Of hearing people talking about;
Problems that no one wants to hear.

Let me get this straight,
I never loved God or Satan,
I just needed company.

Who can honestly say they never needed company?

This Poem Has No Title and No Meaning

She brings me back from the brink,
Reason is dead
But love
Is alive.
All I wanted was someone to hear me,
And now all I want is to die.

No wonder people leave me.

Breeding idiots

Mindless drones, dialling phones.
Eyes glued to shows viewed,
These willing sheep are easy reap
As ratings soar and they want more.

Mindless art, lacking heart,
Innocent guilt is falsely built.
Creating destruction through soulless production,
As listeners soar and they want more.

Dreary eyed and losing pride,
The fleeing heard sees everything blurred,
A clueless reinvention to fund the devils pension.

When everything is one in the same
People, sounds and fashion;
Who is it to blame?
The ugly twisted soul;
Black heart, suit and hair,
Is he not but fulfilling his role?

The blame lies within,
And my patience razor thin.
You watch and laugh,
At how pathetic they all seem,
Yet they sit and laugh at you,
As you fund their twisted scheme.

Yet you're the first to complain;
When everything you see around,
Looks and sounds the same.
Now we're all just getting bored of everything we once adored,
It's such a mess and we want less.

Older and Wiser

Older and wiser,
Love doesn't bless me,
It haunts me.

It stalks me at every turn,
Appearing when I least expect it;
Just as I begin to settle without it;
Just as I think it's gone;
It rears its foul head to haunt me once more;
The ugly devil himself;
I know he laughs when I cry.

What have you ever done for me?
Why do we all seek to find you?
What has love ever done for us?

Yet,
I greet him like an old friend;
I serenade him like a lover;
Who would've thought it?

The ghastly ghoul of love;
He is my lover.

What has love ever done for me?
It brought me my only true love.

In Contradiction

I am no longer scared of love,
A life without love,
Is a life not loved at all.
I was dying to live,
Love set me free,
The façade crumbled,
Under the haze of glory days,
Set my weary love ablaze,
Fear gone without a trace,
I found meaning in a world I had no place.

It gave me a fright,
When our love first took flight,
But now I feel just like a bird.
Did I just write that?
Man,
How absurd.

Foghorns

I missed the foghorns on the river this morning,
It's been quite warm recently,
So it came as a surprise to me that I missed them.

I hate the way they wake me,
I hate the way they sound,
I hate the way they seem to hate me.

I hated them then,
I hate them now,
Yet nothing I have found,
Can replace their unique sound.

They rouse me from my bed,
I stare out of the window,
And listen out to no avail;
Where is my favourite sound?

I must point out I'm not insane,
Just lovesick once again.

Who'd have thought I could miss something that I hate so much?

Proverb

A man who never has his heart broken is a cynic;
A man who has his heart broken once is a learner;
A man who has his heart broken twice is a lover;
A man who has his heart broken more than three times is a fool.

I guess you could say I'm learning?

Soul in a Jar

So, the president's black.
And, that's nice, I guess.
But, haven't they all been black?

For I see not race;
But suits and souls.

Both of which boast expensive price tags;
Both are easily bought, easily sold;
Both are black, empty and cold;

I wouldn't get too excited just yet.

Think

The night is dark but the light goes off in my head. I have stories in my head and sometimes I need to get them out. I can never find enough words. There are not enough words to describe the complexity of the world around us. Every time I try, my voice catches and I fall silent. My voice is silent but my brain never will be.

We can all think.
We can all live.
We can all dream of thinking about living.
I dream of a world where I don't need to live to think.

The Night

The golden silence of the night was broken only by the sound of my own footsteps. It assured me that I was the only certainty in an uncertain world. If there is nothing but me then I am happy in my own company, as anyone should be. But as I walked the streets, disillusioned with everything I knew about myself, I knew I was alone. Entire worlds crumbled around me as I stood still waiting for the bus, her words still ringing in my ears. It wasn't me, it was anybody else, as it was and always will be. Everything has an expiration date, I just didn't realise mine was already up.

Rise & Fall

Beauty weaved on intangible threads;
Wilting golden where she treads;
She made sure my passion stirred;
The most beautiful song you've ever heard;
Surely it cannot be;
That this beautiful song is being sung to me?

My ears ached for the music;
My heart ached for the beauty;
If music is the food of love,
Then my gut shall stay content;
For all the world can but say;
For certain love I never meant.

Happy, healthy, hearty music feeds my heart once more;
My soul is nourished not by the beauty I cannot see,
But the one who once stood in front of me.

Phoenix rise, phoenix die;
This love shall burn forever.
No time shall come when one can't hear,
Our silent golden melody.

Now I see how I was blind;
And given time I found something worth calling mine;
It goes to show,
Life can be kind, sometimes.

Warning

Give yourself to others;
Don't let them take you.
We are our own,
To have and to hold.
At the end of the day,
Who will love you at the end,
That girl who always went away?
For my heart just cannot mend,
What you took from me.

Give yourself to others;
Don't let them take you.
If we hold our own,
There's nothing they can do.
Who will love you at the end
The one who stuck it through?
Do not give yourself to others,
Only you can always be there for you.

Pearl

Flowing locks on grand shoulders;
There are none more beautiful,
Nor bolder.
Tender neck of aches and pains;
Caressed with care;
Make a man feel home again.

A smile shy with eyes so wide;
You catch them staring,
With nowhere to hide.
A single spot of happiness,
Upon a lonely face;
Does nothing but impress.

A heavenly scent;
A charm so wild;
You must be from the angels sent.

Whoever stands by you,
Hand in hand,
Will be the only lucky man.

Look in the mirror,
Smile and say,
We're going to change the world some day.

Unfinished

There are words to perfectly describe,
All the feelings and emotions you could ascribe,
To being nothing but dead inside,

And that is why,
If there ever comes a time,
To decide, whether to fall or to fly,
Choose to fall,
It's easier that way, is all.

Temporary Lover

Winter nights come round again;
So cold and lonely;
Yet filled with joy.
Hearing running water trickle;
Sends shivers down the spines;
Hairs on end,
The mirror, pointlessly fickle.

Biting air and whistling wind;
It catches on the lips,
And inside the gentle ear;
It grasps so tightly;
Gasping, shaking,
Like a lover's touch without the charm.

A darling night,
With love so tight,
Is not at all too wrong.

My love affair with summer waned,
And or some reason unexplained;
I ask,
Winter won't you come again?

A year is far too long.

A Question

When you say mine,
I mean that's fine,
But why?

Why in a world of sculptures,
Would you pick the wrecking ball?
I turn beauty into rubble,
But rising from the ashes,
You're like a phoenix at the double,
You say you appreciate the trouble,
That I cause.
Even though my history is quite profound,
And there is no way around,
That feeling that you have,
Don't get me wrong; I'm glad,
I just don't understand.

Hopefully I'll be OK this time around.

Stories of my Existential Life III: Looking Forward

Looking up at the stars,
Never gave me an answer,
I had to look inside myself,
To find what I feared.

Born alone, die alone,
It's the way that we live,
We've all destroyed God,
We just wanted rid.

Now he's left us to die.

Please come back for me.

Thus ends a tale not worth telling.

www.ingramcontent.com/pod-product-compliance
Lightning Source LLC
Chambersburg PA
CBHW031506040426
42444CB00007B/1225